FALLING ANGEL :
RISING PHOENIX

FALLING ANGEL :
RISING PHOENIX

ANTONIO LIRANZO

Antonio Liranzo

This is for anyone that has ever felt lost, I hope these poems help you find your mission in life.

Contents

Part 1

Fallen Angel

I

Fallen angel

The strength of my wings
As strong as the Earth's core
But somehow
Managing to dismantle.

They say "sticks and stones won't break my bones"
But they don't tell you that cruel people and self sabotage
can break your spirit
It's easy to be a beautiful goddess one day
And a fallen angel the next.

I've built up so much
But suddenly I'm crashing and burning
As I fall and prepare for death
I hope my wings are what's left.

I do believe in destiny and reincarnation

Maybe this fire that I'm in
Can release the ashes
For a phoenix to rise again.

To the world
Sorry for being so weak
As I descend into eternity
I hope my legacy becomes eternal.

Remember
As strong as someone may seem
As high as someone can be
It's easy to hide the truth inside.

Sometimes
Life is a scary rollercoaster ride
Let this be a lesson
To always count your blessings.

Remember as high as you can go
Is as low as you can feel
To be that strong phoenix
You have to trust your inner beauty.

2

Roads

There are three lanes in life
Staying in the middle
I've always played it safe
Because I can't choose a side.

An intersection challenges me
I must change lanes
Looking ahead
Is a sudden decision so bad?

3

Poison

Would you ingest the risk for me?
Swallow, thy says
Internally I think...
Is this risk worth it?

Swallow he says
Internally I think...
The risk
Is he worth it?

4

Bittersweet

Out of breath
Running and crying
Why would you do this to me?
I'm betrayed and hurt.

Will I learn from them?
I will be the light in the dark woods
I refuse to be owned by manipulation
I am bitter but know, once I grow I am living in sweet
dreams.

5

Crocodile tears

Dried out
See no more
My heart in two
The pain I have endured.

No sympathy
Face, stone cold
That Medusa stare
Knows how to make me freeze these tears.

Becoming so numb to the pain
Which you inflicted
Caused obscene anger
Due to you being inflicted.

6

Blue Jay

Mr. Blue where have you been?
You were so cuddly and lovable
Now just a tarnished soul
Mr. Blue where have your feathers gone?

Blue is the color of the ocean
Blue represents cold
Mr. Blue was light as the sky
Mr. Blue was warm like the sun.

Mr. Blue left his nest this morning
The journey? No one knows
Maybe, Blue is somewhere flapping his wings
Mr. Blue can see no harm.

I woke up to a strange bird this morning
One of orange and red feathers
He looked at me as if he knew me already

Those black eyes I can't forget!

Mr.Blue is that you?!

7

This Is Me

Curled up in fetal position
Wondering if I'm ever going to escape
Why did this happen to me?
Someone that just wants to share their love.

Ended up in a dark world
Full of monsters and users
Never before have I met an abuser
Suddenly my life has turned around.

Hitting rock bottom
More like hitting never ending reality
I wanted something pure
Not fatal.

Offering light and love
Swallowed by these demons
I need a candle for my optimism

Lost in this cave of life.

Searching and seeking for a way out
Fighting obstacles and hurdles
My inner goddess has come out
Let darkness become light.

Light be the guidance
To the truth of the universe
My mission is to be free
From the truth that is me.

8

Dark Twisted Fantasy

Gremlins
Ghosts
Vampires
In this dark twisted fantasy.

Vivid dreams
Night terrors
Restless mornings
When will I see the light?!

Overworked and overused
Crashing and burning
When do I learn the fine line?
An incubus sucking the life out of me.

Lifeless in this dark twisted fantasy
A spider with only 6 legs
Sacrificing body parts to be a part of this "fantasy"

Not knowing, this fantasy is a natural disaster.

You live and you learn, right?
Then why is this dark twisted fantasy on repeat?
Like a ghost with a restless soul
I am embodied by the lies of this dark twisted fantasy.

9

Lives

I've lived 1000 lives
I only ever told one lie
Truth be told, I have a devil on my shoulder
But an angel in my eye.

I've been there, I've done that
Oh, "you're still so young"
If you only knew
At this age, I've experienced more than a history book.

That one lie I told
To hide the truth
I was ready for what life was going to give me
But little did I know, I was born to combat this tempting
energy.

I've lived 1000 lives, yet this one makes me feel like I only
have one.

10

WOKE

People don't know the power I harness
Behold the silly side of you
If you only knew
The star power I hold.

Glimmering light
Shimmering night
Phantom lights
Behold the night.

I hold
I take
I ask
I rule.

I state now
Welcome to the world of I
Learn to respect and love thy

Love is the beholder of my eye.

Gas lighting
Instant gratification
Hiding behind messages
Game over for the non woke, of the world that is de-
manding more....

Invisible Poem

Do you see me?
Feeling like a new coat of white paint on a wall
Blind as a bat?
Feeling like a line on a piece of paper.

What we could have is no more
You're oblivious , you can see no more
My signs were strong & real
Your acknowledgment was weak & fake.

I believe in strength and unity
You believe in just using me
I believe in trust and honesty
You believe in hoeing and dishonesty.

I guess wounds do heal
You're on an endless treadmill
I am rising like the sun

While you have your fuck boy fun.

This phoenix has learned his worth
Always know this fire is rebirth.

Part 2

Rising Phoenix

12

New Beginnings

Im soaring
A plane going 500 miles per hour
Where is my destination?
It's called my new life.

I've crashed
I burned
I fell
I lost.

I learned
I searched
I found
I won...

Rising like the sun
This new found love, has awakened my inner solar eclipse
You may want to close your eyes

Because this phoenix is fully equipped.

13

State of mind

Good feelings
Conquering your city
Feeling mighty
You are going to rule your world!

Cloud nine
Feeling like a molly trip
Yet there's no crashing
Who knew you could fly!

Never let go of your dreams
People want to take everything
Greed is cruel
But owning your destiny is beautiful!

14

Cheers to me

Feeling high almighty
So divine
I want to make myself
Mine!

I salute
To the goddess
Within me
From Fire to stars.

Celebrating
Self acceptance
Self Trust
Loneliness.

The inner beauty
Has awaken an energy in me
Who knew that I didn't need you?

This whole time it was me that needed me.

Cheers to me!

15

Feels

Like snow on Christmas
I'm feeling joyful
Like the first beach day of summer
I'm feeling playful.

These feelings are so magical
I must be in a midsummer night dream
Holding me in the park
I feel like a school boy that received a gold star.

Blushing from affection
I finally realized my intention
Dreaming a mile a minute
Who knew you would blow away this cloudy storm.

Epiphany

Epiphanies
Like drugs
Am I hallucinating
On these genuine visions?

That ah-ha moment!
Realizing
Remembering
Conquering.

The enigma that I am
Rehabilitating my spirit
Manifesting a restart
My mission is finally complete.

17

Ruler of the night

Ruler of the night
Enter my limelight
Mixed signals like a yellow traffic light
Head on car collision, I'm feeling like dynamite.

Like mercury in retrograde
I am feeling pulled and lost
But the energy of the moon
Helps me become a creature of the night.

I am a ruler of the night
Lurking around these busy streets
Dodging traffic
Looking for an alternative route.

18

Rolling Through Life

I feel so high and mighty
Like my friend Molly
I roll through the day
Strolling, bypassing and observing.

Who knew being a wallflower, could be so fun
Blending in
Unbothered
Receiving good energy.

I feel inspired
I feel free
Free to love
Free to rediscover.

It's a pinnacle to know who you are
It's important to love yourself
But it's also important...

To have fun.

My hair is loose
My clothes are wrinkled
I am sweating
My heart is racing.

All these thrills
So much excitement
I can't contain
My rising phoenix fire is bursting.

I am ready to ascend
But for these last few moments of observing
I've learned
Maybe the world isn't so bad.

Keep all these lessons learned
For the day that I return
I don't have to return as a fallen angel
But as a loving human.

19

Fresh Air

Bright lights
Circulating moments
Self trust
Forget doubt.

I have a new approach
Why do we always talk about the butterfly?
The caterpillar is a symbol of a slow but worthy journey
Take your time!

Self reminder
Stay positive
Breathe in, breathe out
For this new chapter is as refreshing as fresh air.

Acknowledgements

I want to say thank you to everyone for taking the time to read this book. I have been writing my whole life and have never felt the confidence to release any kind of poetry until now. Writing poetry is one of my forms of expression and I am beyond happy that I get to show the world my emotions and thoughts.

To my editor and proof reader, Viterbo Liranzo, my brother. I am so happy to have worked along with you on this book and have someone give me their opinion on the flow and wording of all my poems.

To everyone that is buying this book and reading my compilation of poems, thank you!

Antonio Liranzo is a performer and writer from New York. He grew up on Long Island and moved to New York City to pursue his dreams to be an artist. This is Antonio's first published book. Writing poetry since he was a child, he always dreamed of having his work published for the public to read and feel the emotions he felt. Antonio has a BA in Communications and Sociology and is obsessed with all things Britney Spears.